101 Christmas Jokes Plus Tongue Twisters

Timothy Hogan

Why did the woman make a Christmas wreath out of Franklin Fir branches? Because she really likes a wreath of Franklin.

Why does Mrs. Claus do her laundry in Tide? Because it's too cold out-tide!

Which one of Santa's reindeer is the cleanest? Comet!

What do you call an elf who doesn't believe in Christmas? A rebel without a Claus.

Why would you invite a mushroom to your Christmas party? He's a fungi to be with.

What nationality is Santa Claus? North Polish.

Knock Knock. Who's there? A Wayne. A Wayne who? A Wayne in a manger...

Why do mummies like Christmas so much? They love all the wrapping.

What do you call someone who's afraid of both Christmas and tight spaces? Santa-Claustrophobic.

Knock, knock Who's there? Atch Atch who? Bless you.

What's so special about Santa tying his tie? It's the knot before Christmas!

Where do snowmen keep their money? In a snowbank.

Why was Santa's little helper sad? Because he had low elf-esteem!

Knock Knock. Who's there? Hannah. Hannah who? Hannah Partridge in a pear tree.

What did the reindeer say to the football player? "Your Blitzen days are over!"

Who brings Christmas presents to all the good dogs? Santa Paws!

What do you call a Christmas tree you forget to water? Nevergreen.

Who lives at the North Pole, makes toys and rides around in a pumpkin? Cinder-elf-a.

How does Santa Claus take a picture? With his North Pole-aroid!

What is the best book to read during the holidays? Harry Potter and the Chamber of Secret Santas.

What's a Christmas tree's least favorite time of year? Sep-timber!

Who is married to Santa's uncle? Auntie Claus.

How does Santa keep his bathroom clean? He uses Comet.

How did Darth Vader know what Luke got him for Christmas? He felt his presents.

What animal loves to go downhill in the snow? A mo-ski-toe.

Why do Dasher and Dancer drink coffee? Because they're Santa's star bucks!

What do snowmen eat for breakfast? Frosted Flakes

When are your eyes not eyes? When winter wind makes them water.

What goes "Oh, oh, oh"? Santa Claus walking backward.

Who delivers Christmas presents to the detective? Santa Clues!

What kind of music do elves like best? Wrap music!

What do you call people interested only in board games at Christmas? Chess nuts roasting by an open fire.

How do you know when it's really cold outside? When you chip a tooth on your soup!

What kind of bike does Santa Claus ride? A Holly Davidson.

What food do you get when you cross Frosty with a wolf? A brrrr-grrr.

Who delivers Christmas gifts to all the good little gazelles? Santelope.

What do rhinos use to decorate their Christmas trees? Hornaments.

What's the difference between Santa Clause and a knight? One slays the dragon, and the other drags the sleigh!

What do you call Santa's little helpers? Subordinate clauses.

Where does Santa sleep when he's traveling? In a ho-ho-hotel.

What's a snowman's favorite dessert? Ice Krispie treats.

What do you call a big brown animal that loves the holidays? A merry Chris-moose.

What do you call someone who gets emotional at Christmastime? Santa-mental.

What's a dog's favorite Christmas carol? Bark, the Herald Angels Sing!

Why did the turkey join the band? Because he had the drumsticks!

How did Scrooge win the football game? The Ghost of Christmas passed.

Knock, knock. Who's there? Needle. Needle who? Needle little money for Christmas presents!

What do you get when you cross a snowman with a vampire? Frostbite!

How do Christmas trees keep their breath fresh? By sucking on orna-mints.

What did Adam say the day before Christmas? "It's Christmas, Eve."

What do you get when you cross Frosty with a baker? Frosty the Dough-man.

What did the Christmas tree say to the ornament? "Don't you get tired of just hanging around?"

What did the gingerbread man put on his bed? A cookie sheet.

What do you get if you cross a pig with a Christmas tree? A porky-pine.

What do you a lobster that won't share its Christmas presents? Shellfish.

What did the ghost say to Santa Claus? I'll have a boo Christmas without you.

What happened to Santa's sleigh in the No Parking zone? It got mistle-towed.

Knock, Knock! Who's there? Dexter. Dexter who? Dexter halls with boughs of holly!

Why did the cat take so long to wrap presents? He wouldn't stop until they were purr-fect.

Why are Christmas trees so bad at sewing? They always drop their needles.

What is Santa called when he takes a rest while delivering presents? Santa Pause!

What's large, green, works in a toy factory and carries a big trunk? An elfant.

If fruit comes from a fruit tree, where does the Christmas turkey come from? A poul-tree.

What is Santa's favorite athletic event? The North Pole-vault.

What illness does Santa try and avoid on Christmas Eve? Shingles.

Knock, knock. Who's there? Tissue. Tissue who? All I want for Christmas tissue...

What did Santa name his reindeer that couldn't stand up straight? Eileen.

What happened when the Christmas turkey got in a fight? He got the stuffing knocked out of him.

What did the dentist see at the North Pole? A molar bear.

What kind of pizza does Good King Wenceslas like best? Deep pan, crisp and even.

Where did Santa learn how to slide down chimneys? At the chimnasium.

How do elves clean the sleigh before Christmas Eve? They use Santa-tizer.

What did Mrs. Claus say when she won the lottery? "Christmas be my lucky day!"

What's an ig? A snow home without a loo.

Why is it so cold during Christmas? Because it's in Decem-brrr!

Why did the Christmas cookie go to the doctor? Because he was feeling crummy.

Why did the Christmas tree go to the barbershop on Christmas Eve? He needed to get trimmed.

What would a reindeer do if she lost her tail? Go to the re-tail shop.

Why does Santa have three gardens? So he can hoe, hoe, hoe!

What is Sherlock's favorite Christmas carol? "I'll be Holmes for Christmas"

Why didn't Rudolph get a good report card? Because he went down in history.

What is Scrooge's favorite board game at Christmas? Mean-opoly!

How does a penguin build a house? Igloos it together.

What do you call a really smart caribou? A brain-deer.

What is Tarzan's favorite Christmas carol? Jungle Bells!

How does a snowman get to work? By icicle.

What's a barber's favorite Christmas song? "Oh Comb All Ye Faithful!"

What do elves do after school? Their gnome work.

What happens if you clap for some holly? It'll take a bough.

Knock, knock. Who's there? Honda. Honda who? Honda first day of Christmas, my true love gave to me...

What did the snowman say to the rude carrot? "Get out of my face!"

What did Santa say to the elf in his workshop who was making a globe? "Small world, isn't it?"

Knock Knock! Who's there? Donut. Donut Who? Donut open 'til Christmas!

What smells most in a chimney? Santa's nose.

Knock, Knock. Who's there? Olive. Olive who? Olive, the other reindeer.

What is a bird's favorite Christmas story? The Finch Who Stole Christmas.

Why should you ask for a broken drum for Christmas? You can't beat it!

What do you call ten rabbits hopping backward through the snow together? A receding hare line.

What is Santa's favorite candy? Jolly Ranchers.

What do you call Santa when he's broke? Saint Nickel-less.

What game do reindeer play in their stalls? Stable-tennis!

Knock, knock. Who's there? Emma. Emma who? Emma freezing out here, let me in!

Tongue Twisters –
Say Them Five Times Fast!

Santa stuffs Stephanie's striped stocking.

Santa Clause's cloak closes tightly.

Rudolph runs rings 'round Rover.

Santa's seven sleighs slid sideways.

Bobby brings bright bells.

Ten tiny tin trains toot ten times.

Tiny Tim trims tall trees with tinsel.

How many deer would a reindeer reign if a reindeer could reign deer?

Silly smelly snowman slips and slides

Eight elves eagerly ate everything.

Santa's Short Suit Shrunk.

Kris Kringle climbs
Christmas chimneys.

Comet cuddles cute
Christmas kittens carefully.

Eleven elves licked eleven
little licorice lollipops.

Chilly chipper children
cheerfully chant.

Kris Kringle clapped crisply.

There's chimney soot on Santa's suit.

Running reindeer romp 'round red wreaths.

Crazy kids clamor for candy canes and Christmas cookies.

Santa's sleigh slides on slick snow.

Cookies crumbling can cause Christmas grumbling.

Printed in Great Britain
by Amazon

34304630R00022